PYTHONS

THE SNAKE DISCOVERY LIBRARY

Sherie Bargar   Linda Johnson

Photographer/Consultant: George Van Horn

Rourke Enterprises, Inc.
Vero Beach, Florida 32964

Library of Congress Cataloging in Publication Data

Bargar, Sherie, 1944-
 Pythons.

 (The Snake discovery library)
 Includes index.
 Summary: Introduces the nonpoisonous python—one
of the world's largest snakes, which may grow to a
length of thirty-three feet.
 1. Pythons—Juvenile literature. [1. Pythons.
2. Snakes] I. Johnson, Linda, 1947- . II. Van Horn,
George, ill. III. Title. IV. Series: Bargar,
Sherie, 1944- . Snake discovery library.
QL666.063B38 1987   597.96   87-12689
ISBN 0-86592-244-6

Title Photo:
Ball Python
Python regius

TABLE OF CONTENTS

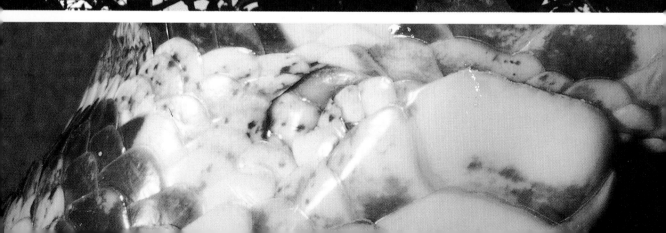

Asian Reticulated Python
Python reticulatus

PYTHONS

The nonpoisonous python, a member of the *Pythonidae* family, is among the world's largest snakes and most powerful constrictors. An adult Asian Reticulated Python may be 33 feet long which is about the length of a school bus. The African Python may be 25 feet long which is about the length of a garage. Through the ages snakes lost their need for legs because they began to live underground. Today the python still has parts of its pelvis which is evidence of its **ancestral** legs. Another sign of its past is the horny claws which are seen where its legs used to be. This is why the python is one of the world's most primitive snakes.

Spur of Burmese Python
  Python molurus biuitatus

WHERE THEY LIVE

Tropical climates with heavy rainfall which create forests of dense growth are the homes of most species of pythons. These climates are found in Southeastern Asia, the East Indies, Africa, Australia, Central America, and India. Some species prefer the dry desert climate while others live in high mountainous regions or grassy rolling plains. Most large pythons are ground dwellers but easily climb trees and are excellent swimmers. One well-developed lung contributes to its swimming ability.

New Guinea Tree Python
Chondropython viridis

HOW THEY LOOK

Smooth shiny scales cover the heavy-bodied python which ranges in length from 8 to 33 feet depending on the species. Although some adult pythons have been known to weigh 300 pounds, the average adult Burmese Python weighs about 100 pounds. Other adult species like the Ball Python may weigh only 5 pounds. The python's muscular body moves slowly, but more silently than other large land animals. **Interweaving** patterns of yellow, brown, gray, white, and black encircle the Reticulated Python. A well-developed head of uniform brown has a narrow black line from the eye to the neck. Other species are represented by a wide variety of patterns and colors.

9

Burmese Python
Python molurus biuitatus

THEIR SENSES

Sighting the motion of potential **prey**, an extremely hungry python attacks immediately and discovers what it has caught only after the kill. A less hungry python flicks out its tongue to decide if the moving object is an appropriate meal. The tongue helps make this decision by bringing in particles to the Jacobson's organ in the roof of the snake's mouth. The Jacobson's organ **analyzes** the particles quickly. This information is coupled with the heat receptors locating the body warmth of the potential **prey**. If the senses determine that **prey** is near, the kill follows rapidly. This entire process takes only a few seconds.

Reticulated Python
Python reticulatus

Seizing duck by head

Constricting duck

Using windpipe for air while swallowing duck.

Reticulated Python
Swallowing Its Prey.

Jaws stretching to swallow largest
part of duck.

Swallowing and shaping duck

Finishing the meal

THE HEAD AND MOUTH

Powerful jaw muscles mark the distinct head of the python. Highly sensitive heat receptor pits are located around the outer edges of the upper and lower jaws. The **nonvenomous** python has no fangs. Instead it has long needle-like teeth. The snake's mouth has 6 rows of teeth. The lower jaw has 2 rows, and the upper jaw has 4. The teeth are curved inward to deliver a firm grip on the **prey** and anchor the snake during constriction. As the python grips its **prey**, the victim struggles for its freedom. This struggle only causes the python's long, curved teeth to become more deeply imbedded in the victim's body.

Burmese Python
Python molurus biuitatus

Heat
Receptors

Teeth

Windpipe

Teeth

BABY PYTHONS

Up to 100 eggs are laid in a single **clutch**. The mother's coiled body protects her eggs and controls the temperature around them. Some species use changes in body chemistry and muscle contractions to warm their eggs while other species use solar energy. The female python remains with her eggs until they hatch in about 2 months. Each baby python **pips** its leathery egg with its **egg tooth** and immediately begins to take care of itself. At birth the baby Reticulated Python weighs 4 ounces and is about 25 inches long.

Reticulated Python laying eggs
Python reticulatus

PREY

A python lies in wait to ambush **prey**. Seizing the **prey** by its head, it wraps around the **prey** animal. The victim is not crushed, but firmly held in place. The coils of the python tighten around the **prey's** chest each time it breathes out. This stops the **prey** from being able to breathe, and it **suffocates**. This method of killing is constriction. Pythons prefer to feed on mammals and birds. A large python can swallow **prey** weighing up to 100 pounds but usually feeds on a large number of smaller animals. Young pythons have many enemies, but as they grow larger, fewer animals can kill them.

Burmese Python swallowing rabbit
Python molurus biuitatus

THEIR DEFENSE

Camouflage and the ability to hide are the primary defenses of the python. The West African Ball Python coils into a round ball when frightened. It tucks its head and neck into spaces between the folds so it can be pushed 10 to 12 feet like a large bowling ball. The Calabar Ground Python uses this same defense behavior. It also moves around on the ground with its head pointed down and its tail up to confuse its enemies. When attacked by an enemy, a python fights savagely. When defending itself, a python seizes the enemy with its long piercing teeth. Without releasing the grip, the python rips through the flesh of its enemy.

Ball Python
Python regiu.

PYTHONS AND PEOPLE

Rodents, which would destroy farmers' crops, are eaten by pythons. Actually, pythons devour tons of rodents annually. In Asia python meat is eaten and considered a delicacy by many. Python skins have been an important influence in the fashion industry. Even today the complicated patterns of their skin are recreated for clothing.

GLOSSARY

analyze (AN a lyze) analyzes — To find out what something is.

ancestral (an CES tral) — Past generations.

camouflage (CAM ou flage) — The color of an animal's skin that matches the ground around it.

clutch (CLUTCH) — A group of snake eggs.

egg tooth (EGG TOOTH) — A temporary tiny ridge which is very sharp and used to open the egg. It is on the top of a baby snake's nose.

interweave (in ter WEAVE) interweaving — Lines of color that cross over each other.

nonvenomous (non VEN om ous) — Does not cause sickness or death.

pip (PIP) pips — The first opening made by an animal hatching from an egg.

prey (PREY) — An animal hunted or killed by another animal for food.

suffocate (SUF fo cate) suffocates — To kill by not allowing an animal to breathe.

INDEX